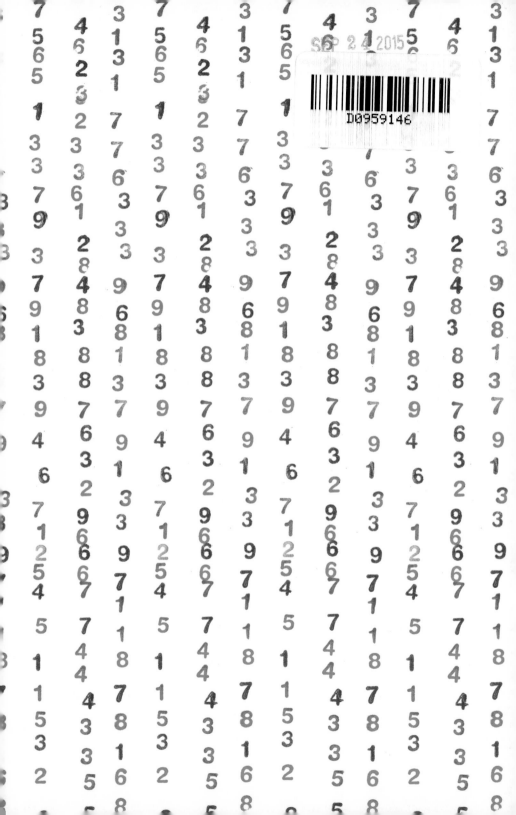

*The Ghost of Karl Marx*

*For little Coco*

# The Ghost of
# Karl Marx

Narrated by
Ronan de Calan

Illustrated by
Donatien Mary

Translated by
Anna Street

*Plato & Co.*
diaphanes

*A phantom haunts Europe...*

*Guten Tag!* Good Day! Don't be afraid, it's only a sheet!
My name is Karl Marx. I'm no spring chicken; pretty soon
I'll celebrate my 200th birthday! But don't think that I died in
order to be roaming around like a ghost! Don't believe those
who say that and who love repeating it. It's me alright, in flesh
and blood, all of me blood and flesh hidden under a sheet!
The sheet is to trick those who only recently were chasing me,
for all the European nations conspired to organize a sacred
hunt with me as the prize catch!

That's why I had to flee, just as the hare abandons his
burrow sniffed out by dogs, from Berlin to Paris, from Paris
to Brussels, from Brussels to London, always escaping my
pursuers. But nowadays, this sheet mostly works to scare
them, as you shall see!
They think I'm dead and fear my ghost...

What am I doing under this sheet? Well, it's a long story, one about the class struggle. A sad story, but one to which we are going and try to give a happy ending, a joyful outcome, for what would be the point of inventing endings if we can't make them happy!

This story begins a few years before my birth, in the region with the pretty name of Silesia, then a region of Germany, my home country. Poor peasant families in Silesia who had recently escaped the domination of greedy and lazy lords farmed their own plots of land as free men and sold their wheat in town.

Then one day when they went into town to sell their wheat, the merchant told them:

*"Your wheat is too expensive! The farmers of Westphalia, who use the new farming machines, sell it to me for less. From now on I will buy from them, not from you! Don't look at me like that: it is not my fault; these are the rules of the Market!"*

The peasants of Silesia went home greatly angered, and in the following months, they were reduced to eating all of their wheat. The year after that, since there was no money to buy seeds and replant their crops, they had to sell their homes.

When the contractor arrived to buy their homes, he told them:

*"Your homes are too expensive! The farmers of Pomerania, who have also abandoned their fields, sell their houses to me for less. What's more, nobody wants these hovels! Take these few coins for your homes, and go look for work in town! And don't look at me like that, it's not my fault, it's the law of the Market!"*

And so the peasants of Silesia went to town, for sooner or later almost everybody ends up in a town. Owning almost nothing, they brought almost nothing: their linen, a few pieces of furniture and the old weaving looms they used to make clothing and sheets from flax or cotton.

And this is how, in town, they became at-home weavers, or, to be precise, cloth manufacturers. Night and day, they wove and wove and, as the months and years went by, managed to feed their families, put a roof over their heads, buy furniture and regain hope. But one fine day, the clothing merchant to whom they sold their fabrics told them:

*"Your cloth is too expensive! The cloth factories of Franconia sell me their fabrics for less! From now on, I'm going to buy from them, not from you. As for yourselves, go ask for a job at the factory. And don't look at me like that: I have nothing to do with your problems; these are the hard facts of the Market!"*

13

In despair, the weavers of Silesia went to the cloth factory. As they arrived, they saw a huge crowd in front of the buildings: peasants such as themselves, who had been forced to leave their land, small craftsmen ruined by the factory, young people who had squandered their meager fortune, and even small merchants who hadn't understood the rules of the Market. All came to swell the ranks of this working class that we call the proletariat, these people who had nothing left to sell for a livelihood except their labor, the strength of their arms.

15

A foreman in charge of hiring stood before them on a platform. He addressed them with a powerful and self-assured voice:

*"There are way too many of you, we do not need all these workers. So we will hire only those who will work for the lowest wage. From now on we will deal only with them, not with anyone else. Make your offers and do not look at me like that. It's not my fault; this is the way the Market works!"*

The first worker, rather elderly, proposed a very low wage for his declining strength. Then came a young man, stronger but starving, who proposed an even lower wage, at a ridiculously low price. And then a third brought his children forward and said that he offered them free of charge as additional workers if they would hire him. It was a contest of who would work the most in order to earn the least!

This is when the weavers became fed up. They had had enough of this Market of which they knew nothing but which had, like a magician evoking the furies of hell, stolen their fields, their homes, their work, and now wanted to steal their bodies and their strength. Since they didn't know against whom they should turn their rage, they decided to take it out first of all on the platform where the foreman was standing, who, scared, ran away. Then they entered the cloth factory, broke the machines used to make cheaper cloth and rendered them useless. In their anger, they set fire to the cloth. Right when the sparks were flying into the air, the revolting weavers realized they were completely surrounded by soldiers with rifles pointed straight at them.

The foreman had run to warn the master, who had warned the factory manager, who had gone to warn the authorities, who had rushed to warn the King himself, and the King had said:

*"Petty weavers, home-spun drapers want to destroy a factory that does not belong to them. They challenge – what am I saying – they violate ownership, which is the foundation of our modern society, our Market society! They must be stopped! Order our army's soldiers to disperse these rebels or to arrest them and, if they refuse, to open fire! Tell them also that it is not only by order of the King, but of the Market itself!"*

And so the soldiers surrounded the factory in defense of the
Market and of private property. Seeing this, the weavers turned
violently against the soldiers, hoping to finally engage in an
open struggle against the Market and its invisible agents, a class
of exploiters who were, for once, represented, personified by
the army. For this is how the class struggle goes: one never
knows exactly whom to fight in order to win, and one often
mistakes one's enemies.

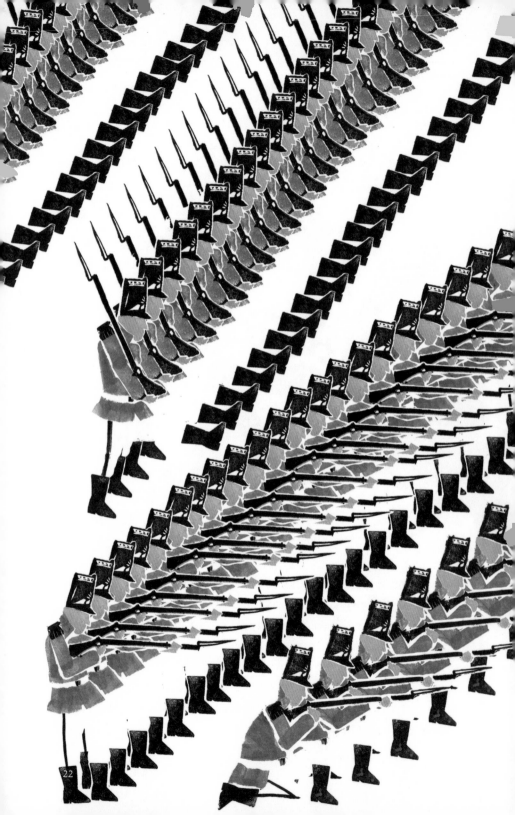

But what could starving weavers do against armed soldiers who had been given orders to shoot, and moreover, in the name of the Market?

I, Karl Marx, young philosophy student newly arrived in town, was near the factory on that particular morning, and I saw the weavers fall under the soldiers' bullets. After having taken their land, exiled, ruined and exploited them, the Market ended up by taking their lives. So before this sad scene, I set a categorical imperative for myself, as in the philosopher Kant's expression, I solemnly vowed to devote the rest of my life to overturning that which renders a human being a thing to be humiliated, enslaved, abandoned, and despised. More than anything, I swore to find the Market, that infernal magician, and to get rid of him once and for all, for the good of everyone. So that I would never forget my vow, I snatched a sheet that had fallen to the ground in this unfair struggle, a sheet from the weavers of Silesia! I took it with me in order to remember them. Today I use it to hide under when I am chased, or to scare my pursuers.

Now that you know the sad story of the Silesian weavers, this horrible example of the class struggle, let's give it a joyful outcome, a happy ending. Let's lead the charge against the Market!

But what is to be done? And moreover, where should we begin? Let's go take a walk around the market, in the ordinary sense of the word. At the market on Festival Square, for example, you can find a bit of everything: fish, meat, fruit and vegetables, furniture and toys. Obviously, the Festival Square market is not, of course, the Market we are looking for! But since we use the same word to designate what goes on every Friday on Festival Square, which seems quite innocent, and the infernal magician who steals lands, homes, enslaves bodies and kills weavers, there must be a connection between them, and I do believe I've found it!

Sitting on a terrace, *Das Kapital* is drinking his coffee.
He looks elegant, polite and kind, some even say he has a
heart of gold, like his watch. I would like to believe that,
but we shall see that things are, as always, more complicated
when the Market joins the dance.

For the moment, leave *Das Kapital* to quietly finish his coffee,
we'll come back to him later.

So then, what do you see in this market? *A vast stockpile of goods*, that's what you see. Each piece of merchandise has its purpose, its use value: the fruit and vegetables, the meat and the fish are meant to be eaten...

or at least, that's the best use that can be made of them! The wicker chairs are meant to be sat in, that is their use, the toy to be played with, this is also its use. From this point of view, all this merchandise has different use values, sometimes they are quite difficult to compare. Hamburger meat can be played with, but it won't last very long. One can try to eat toys, but they are not particularly nourishing and they might break one's teeth! Each item has very different purposes. But if we call all these things merchandise, it is not in relation to their use; it is first of all because they are for sale.

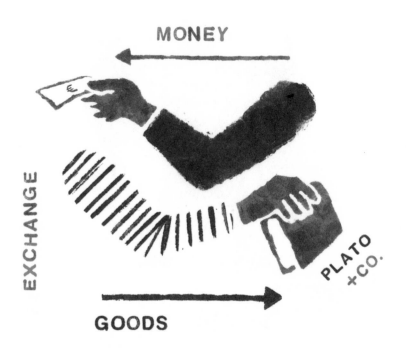

MONEY

EXCHANGE

GOODS

PLATO
+CO.

WATCH     MATCH     MEDICINE

PAINTING     KNIFE     BICYCLE

GASOLINE     FIREARM     MEAT

HAMMER     PEAR     ROLLER-SKATE

Now if you walk closer to the merchandise, you will see that next to each item is marked a *price*. A kilo of potatoes costs one heavy coin, this toy ten coins, this wicker chair fifty coins or a note. But, what is a price?

It is a certain sum of money, of this we are sure. Dig deeper, for we must uncover the mysteries of the Market! Try to remember: what is money really? Coins and notes, certainly, made of more-or-less precious metal, or simply printed paper. Such metal or paper is worthless except for buying things. It has no value except use value, to be exchanged for a certain amount of merchandise.

Someone must have told you, that one does not play with money, nor does one "throw it out of the window." It is used to purchase merchandise. And money can purchase different items: potatoes, toys or chairs; money is the *universal equivalent* of these different pieces of merchandise. The Festival Square market is thus the place where cash is exchanged for merchandise. It seems to me that you have already picked up on this!

1. CUT OUT

Yet once we have said all this, we aren't much closer to
understanding the price for each item of merchandise.
Why does a kilo of potatoes cost a heavy coin and one wicker
chair fifty coins or a note? Is it the use of the merchandise
that decides its price? If that were the case, the price of
merchandise would constantly vary in relation to what people
would consider useful at this or that moment in their life! For
example, hamburger meat is worth a hundred times more to a
hungry person than a wicker chair would be, a toy one thousand
times more valuable to a child than a kilogram of potatoes.
No, the price of merchandise cannot depend upon its use.
Does it not rather depend on the work that is necessary for
its production? This is what I call the *labor theory of value*: the
price of a piece of merchandise, and more generally speaking,
 its exchange value, reflects the amount of labor needed
to produce it.

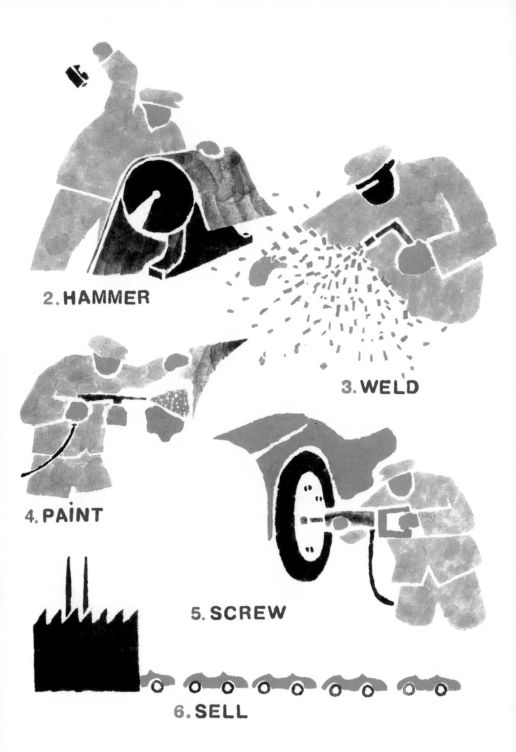

2. HAMMER

3. WELD

4. PAINT

5. SCREW

6. SELL

The face of the Festival Square market has strangely changed: here one does not simply exchange merchandise for cash, but the equivalent of a certain amount of labor, represented by money, for the equivalent of another, represented by merchandise. The famous Market that we are looking for thus depends directly upon the conditions under which we labor, or the *modes of production*. So we must leave the Festival Square market where things are sold, and go and visit the factory where things are produced.

Hey look, *Das Kapital* has just finished his coffee and is headed
for his factory. Let's follow him!

Here we are in his office, this is where *Das Kapital* meets with workers that the foreman has carefully chosen because they work for the least amount of pay. Here comes a worker who must sign his work contract. Let's listen to them, this is called "negotiating," but as you will see in this case, one never really "negotiates": *Das Kapital* dictates his conditions.

"Mister Director, you must help me!" says the worker. "I took this job at the lowest pay because I am in need of everything. My wife is sick in bed and our children are hungry. I already negotiated with your foreman, but I need a small advance on my pay, I beg of you!"

*But my dear man,* replies *Das Kapital, you cannot ignore the rules of the Market. If you cannot properly raise them, why have children? Am I responsible for your situation?*

"Everything was going fine up until now, Mister Director, I was a small business owner, I sold straw-bottomed chairs that I made myself, but the chair factory ruined me by selling its merchandise at a lower price!"

41

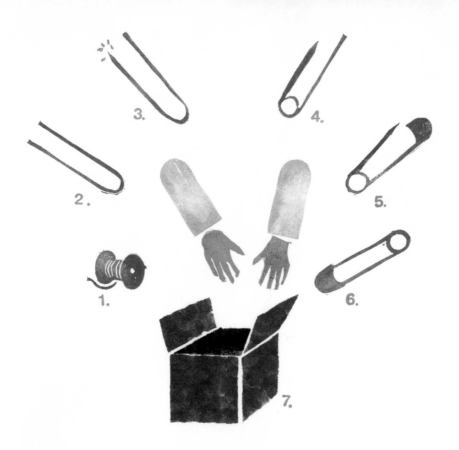

What's your problem? These are the rules of the Market...
Let me explain something to you. My father's father was a small
businessman, just like yourself. But he was very interested in the
means of production. At that time, he made and sold safety pins.
His labor was very specialized: he had to take a spool of wire, pull
the right length of wire from the spool, straighten it, cut it, peak it,
which is to say fashion the tip of the pin, then flatten the other end
and make what is called the head of the pin. This series of tasks was
so time-consuming for him alone that he only managed to produce
around twenty safety pins per day, and his workers even fewer.

But he soon understood that the work can be broken down into single steps in order to save time and thus money. Each worker was assigned a task: one worker unwound the wire from the spool, another straightened it up, a third cut it, a forth peaked it, a fifth was designated to flatten the other end, a sixth struck the head, a seventh bleached the pin, and the last worker placed the pins in their box. The idea of the division of labor was brilliant and yet simple! With the steps organized in this fashion, we were able to produce several hundred pins a day, and to sell many more of them and to make much more money as well. Each worker had a very modest and very simple task to perform that he could repeat mechanically.

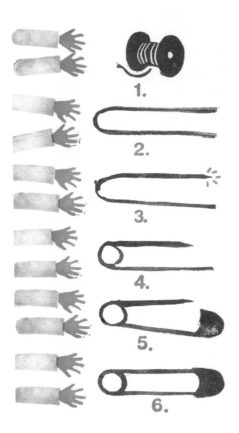

Several years later, when my father took over what had become a pin factory, a British engineer invented a machine that produced pins automatically. We didn't need more than two workers then, one to feed the wire into the machine, and the second to place the machine-made pins into their box. And the machine made over ten thousand safety pins per day! The excess workers were sent away, and my father kept only those who accepted the lowest wage.

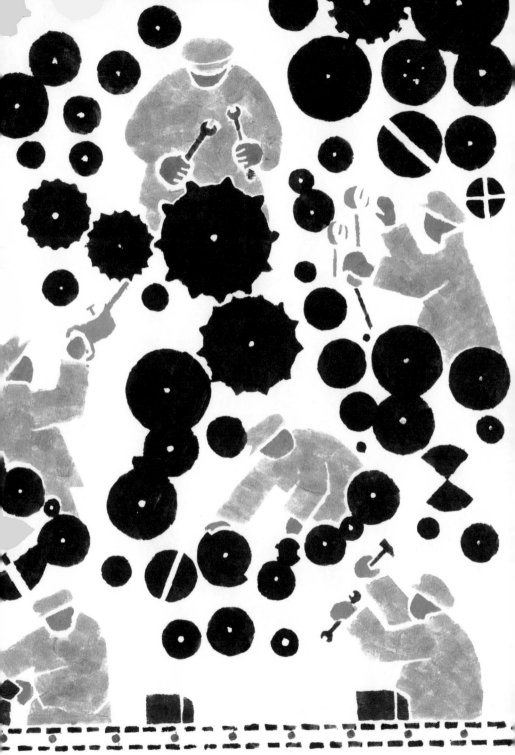

Any worker unhappy about or angered by this very simple and
very repetitive work could simply leave: as his task was not at all
specialized, anybody could replace him, and a great many were
waiting outside, since the machines had replaced hands.
As you demonstrate so beautifully yourself, when it comes to
hiring, it is willingness that prevails, meaning the willingness
to work harder than another laborer who also wants the job!

"But Mister Director," said the worker, "is it not possible to pay your employees a bit more? Or at least to let them take short breaks, for according to what I've been told, the pace of work is relentless here!"

*Dear friend, it is not I who decide the price or the duration of your efforts, it is you! As for me, I am simply the owner of the means of production, in other words of the factory and its machines. You come to me to sell your labor, the strength of your arms. Just like anyone in a market, I buy the labor that is sold to me at the lowest price, it's completely natural! When you buy apples, you buy the cheaper ones, don't you? It's the same with me and your labor power!*

*So if you are not pleased, you can show yourself to the door. Plenty more are waiting outside the door - willing workers, and perhaps more willing than you?*

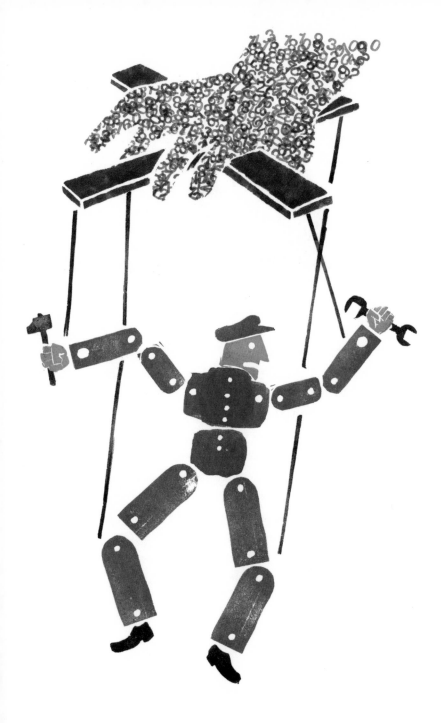

49

What do you think of all of this? I think we have heard
enough: the Market is the place where the workers, the
producers, have to sell their labor at the lowest bid to the
one who owns the essentials, that is to say, the means of
production. The Market is thus not a magician, but simply
theexplanation of a mode of production, a mode where labor
is the merchandise, a mode where the highest-bidding worker
is the one who works the most, meaning the longest, in order
to earn the least, and to allow the owner of the means of
production to earn even more!
So let's ride to the rescue of this exploited worker!
We'll put the sheet back on and pretend to be a ghost.

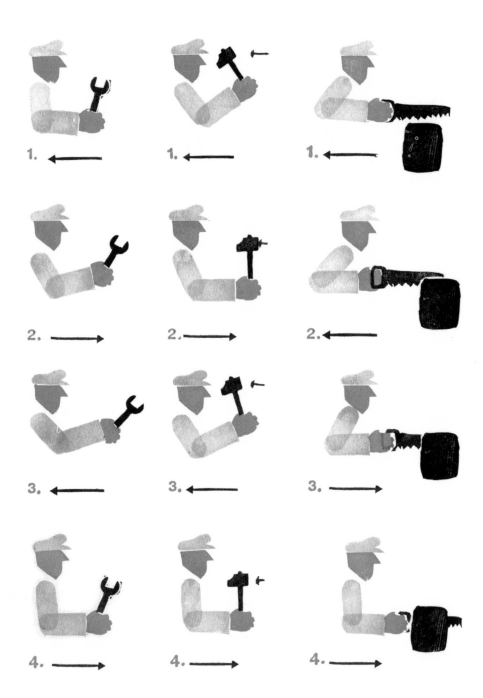

1. ←

1. ←

1. ←

2. →

2. →

2. ←

3. ←

3. ←

3. →

4. →

4. →

4. →

51

*Aaaahhh, help, help, the specter of Marx has come to haunt me!*
*Get thee hence, Communist!*

"Now, now, *Kapital*, don't be ridiculous, by coming to
the rescue of this poor worker, I am actually saving you.
For this situation cannot last! You know very well that one
day starving and outraged workers will come for you, and on
that day, if it comes, I wouldn't want to be in your shoes
for anything in the world... Stop concealing yourself behind
this Evil Genius that is called the Market. You see very well
that the Market is nowhere else than in this unjust contract
that you are trying to get the worker to sign."

*But if he accepts, it frankly isn't my fault!*

"What you say is deeply shocking, but not completely
false. Mister Worker, you must refuse this unjust situation,
not individually, for there will always be someone
poorer or more desperate than you to take your place,
but collectively!"

"But, Mister Ghost, what do you propose I do?"

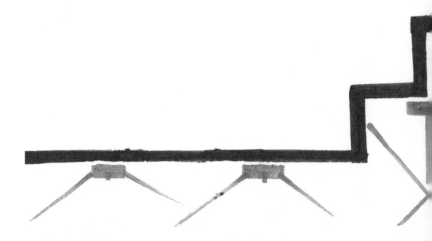

"My solution is, well, somewhat radical, but proportionate to the harm done. Since the injustice of the contract derives from the initial injustice of property, for some have it all, and others have nothing but their own labor to sell, I propose quite simply to abolish private property!"

*Hee, hee, hee,* sniggered *Das Kapital, you are utterly irresponsible, my dear friend!*

"If being responsible means accepting the exploitation of the many by the few, then I do wish to be irresponsible. But listen to me instead: it will be up to the proletariat, meaning the mass of exploited workers, to abolish property. Once private property is abolished, each person will be free in the proper sense of the word, and no longer only free to enslave himself, to become the mere extension of a machine for a miserable wage! Each one will contribute to the well-being of all without submission to another, for society as a whole will regulate general production, not a few persons aiming to make a private profit. For most of one's time, once the necessary social tasks are accomplished – those which allow everyone to feed himself, have a roof over his head, and receive education – each person will be able to do whatever he desires: invent, read, create, fish or hunt in the mornings, breed cattle in the afternoons and practice philosophy in the evenings, according to one's own liking!"

*You are an idealist; that will never work!*
retorted *Das Kapital.*

"Perhaps, but isn't freeing mankind from his shackles the only thing worth trying?"

"I understand you," said the worker, "and I will discuss your ideas with my fellow workers, those who, like me, have nothing."

*Alright then, go ahead, swap your ideas!* Das Kapital *mumbled with an evil grin. In the meantime, there will still be a few responsible men such as myself to produce merchandise-cheaply, as everyone wants... You speak of equality, while I am producing abundance!*

"Abundance in exchange for equality! But abundance for whom, then? Watch out, Mister *Das Kapital*," said the worker, "you'd better think carefully, 'cause if you change your mind too late, there will be nothing left to save you except your own two legs... and you might have to run like mad!"

Okay then! Let's leave *Das Kapital* and the worker and move on, I can see that things are progressing! But let's not celebrate too soon; this disruption of our entire value system is going to require considerable effort, on everyone's part! For it is not merely a matter of overturning injustice by exploiting those who used to be the exploiters, but to do away with exploitation altogether!

59

I'll be back soon to harry *Das Kapital* and his workers,
for this is my calling: to come back and haunt the world,
to try and unite it around my radical solutions!
But for now, I must leave you, my companion on this
adventure, but don't forget our vow, which you share with
me from now on: to overturn all that renders a human being
a thing to be humiliated, enslaved, abandoned, or despised!
Take this piece of cloth from the Silesian weavers:
it will remind you of our vow! Now I must take my leave...

Where am I going? I am boarding this ship, headed for the United States of America! I have a date with...

*Miss Wall Street Panic!*

*French edition*
Ronan de Calan & Donatien Mary:
*Le fantôme de Karl Marx*
Design: Yohanna Nguyen
© Les petits Platons, Paris 2012

First edition
ISBN 978-3-03734-545-0
© diaphanes, Zurich-Berlin 2015

www.platoandco.net
www.diaphanes.com

Layout: 2edit, Zurich
Printed and bound in Germany

| | | | | | | | | | | |
|---|---|---|---|---|---|---|---|---|---|---|
| 7 | 4 | 3 | 7 | 4 | 3 | 7 | 4 | 3 | 7 | 3 | 7 |
| 5 | 6 | 1 | 5 | 6 | 1 | 5 | 6 | 1 | 5 | 1 | 5 |
| 6 | 2 | 3 | 6 | 2 | 3 | 6 | 2 | 3 | 6 | 3 | 6 |
| 5 | 3 | 1 | 5 | 3 | 1 | 5 | 3 | 1 | 5 | 1 | 5 |
| 1 | 2 | 7 | 1 | 2 | 7 | 1 | 2 | 7 | 1 | 7 | 1 |
| 3 | 3 | 7 | 3 | 3 | 7 | 3 | 3 | 7 | 3 | 7 | 3 |
| 3 | 3 | 6 | 3 | 3 | 6 | 3 | 3 | 6 | 3 | 6 | 3 |
| 7 | 6 | 3 | 7 | 6 | 3 | 7 | 6 | 3 | 7 | 3 | 7 |
| 9 | 1 | 3 | 9 | 1 | 3 | 9 | 1 | 3 | 9 | 3 | 9 |
| 3 | 2 | 3 | 3 | 2 | 3 | 3 | 2 | 3 | 3 | 3 | 3 |
| 7 | 8 | 9 | 7 | 8 | 9 | 7 | 8 | 9 | 7 | 9 | 7 |
| 9 | 4 | 6 | 9 | 4 | 6 | 9 | 4 | 6 | 9 | 6 | 9 |
| 1 | 8 | 8 | 1 | 8 | 8 | 1 | 8 | 8 | 1 | 8 | 1 |
| 8 | 3 | 1 | 8 | 3 | 1 | 8 | 3 | 1 | 8 | 1 | 8 |
| 3 | 8 | 3 | 3 | 8 | 3 | 3 | 8 | 3 | 3 | 3 | 3 |
| 9 | 8 | 7 | 9 | 7 | 9 | 9 | 8 | 7 | 9 | 7 | 9 |
| 4 | 7 | 9 | 4 | 6 | 4 | 4 | 7 | 9 | 4 | 9 | 4 |
| 6 | 6 | 1 | 6 | 3 | 6 | 6 | 6 | 1 | 6 | 1 | 6 |
| 7 | 3 | 3 | 7 | 2 | 7 | 7 | 3 | 3 | 7 | 3 | 7 |
| 1 | 2 | 3 | 1 | 9 | 1 | 1 | 2 | 3 | 1 | 3 | 1 |
| 2 | 9 | 9 | 2 | 6 | 2 | 2 | 9 | 9 | 2 | 9 | 2 |
| 5 | 6 | 7 | 5 | 6 | 5 | 5 | 6 | 7 | 5 | 7 | 5 |
| 4 | 6 | 1 | 4 | 7 | 4 | 4 | 6 | 1 | 4 | 1 | 4 |
| 5 | 7 | 1 | 5 | 7 | 5 | 5 | 7 | 1 | 5 | 1 | 5 |
| 1 | 4 | 8 | 1 | 4 | 1 | 1 | 4 | 8 | 1 | 8 | 1 |
| 1 | 4 | 7 | 1 | 4 | 7 | 1 | 4 | 7 | 1 | 7 | 1 |
| 5 | 3 | 8 | 5 | 3 | 8 | 5 | 3 | 8 | 5 | 8 | 5 |
| 3 | 3 | 1 | 3 | 3 | 1 | 3 | 3 | 1 | 3 | 1 | 3 |
| 2 | 5 | 6 | 2 | 5 | 6 | 2 | 5 | 6 | 2 | 6 | 2 |